I0468344

Trucking Accidents in Ohio

What You Need to Know If You Are Injured in a Truck Accident and What You Can Do about It

Slater & Zurz LLP, Attorneys at Law
Serving Clients Throughout Ohio
Office Locations:
Akron • Canton • Cleveland • Columbus

Trucking Accidents in Ohio
By: Slater & Zurz LLP
Attorneys at Law

Table of Contents

Introduction

Unfortunately, when there is a crash between a car and a truck, the car driver and his or her passengers are usually the people seriously injured or killed. The sheer weight of a truck is overwhelming and there is little chance one will just walk away from the accident.

Some truck drivers cannot meet their delivery times and must cheat on their logs to make a living. Others realize such misrepresentation is against federal regulation and will not compromise their job. Because many people believe some truck drivers suffer from fatigue, they assume truck drivers must be the ones at fault in an accident. The truck driver has been found to be at fault in less than 35% of accidents. (Ohio Department of Safety, 2013 statistics).

For more than 40 years, Slater & Zurz LLP has been helping victims who have been wronged and injured by others. The firm will take aggressive action against any insurance company who is trying to minimize payment or outright deny rightful compensation to a Slater & Zurz LLP client.

This book will provide some statistics concerning truck accidents in Ohio and some figures that have been compiled nationally. It will discuss safety regulations that all truckers are expected to follow as part of state and federal law.

If you have ever wondered about how the trucking industry works, this book will give you an overview of the movement of freight in this country. What is being moved, who is doing the moving, what type of trucks are doing the moving, who regulates the industry, what those regulations are and how a driver can be disqualified are all discussed in Chapter 1.

Chapter 2 is devoted to truck accidents. It begins with some accident statistics and then details what happens after a truck accident as the investigation proceeds and evidence is gathered. The chapter concludes by explaining various theories of liability in a truck accident.

Chapter 4 also discusses truck accidents from the legal vantage point of how a truck accident case is conducted from complaint through discovery. It emphasizes the importance of experts, driver logs and preserving important video, audio and computer evidence.

Chapter 3 explains various aspects of insurance coverage for truckers and how coverage is different from that held on most passenger cars. Minimum insurance requirements for the various weights and types of trucks are listed and terms such as "umbrella insurance," "captive coverage" and "reinsurance" are defined.

Many times, being in an accident with a truck will mean your life has been seriously disrupted, perhaps disrupted forever. A person may be brain-damaged or confined to a wheelchair. This is not a time for you or your family to be hesitant about filing a lawsuit or to let the opposing side intimidate you into not acting.

You may have considerable expenses for the rest of your life. You have the right to seek compensation to help you and your family cope with what lies ahead. Slater & Zurz LLP can help you be successful in the quest to be treated fairly.

This book is designed to help you realize there are attorneys out there who are willing to help you when you have been injured by the negligent actions of another party or parties.

Slater & Zurz LLP offers free initial consultations. If we accept your case, it will be done on a contingency fee basis. This means our firm will receive a portion of any award or settlement obtained on your behalf. If there is no recovery, you will not owe any fee.

Slater & Zurz LLP
Call us for a free consultation
1-800-297-9191
slaterzurz.com

DISCLAIMER

The information contained within this book is for informational use only.

This book is not intended to be used as legal advice. No attorney-client relationship has been created or formed because of your receiving, purchasing, or reading this book.

Cases involving trucking accidents are unique, complex, and involve many different legal issues. The outcome of the case is dependent on the unique details of that specific case.

You should consult with a qualified Ohio attorney who is licensed and who has experience with trucking accident cases in the state of Ohio.

If you would like a free consultation with an attorney at the Ohio law firm of Slater & Zurz LLP, please call us at 1-800-297-9191 or visit slaterzurz.com and send a message from our website.

Chapter 1
Trucking Industry Overview

Nearly 70% of all freight moved in the United States moves on trucks. The volume of freight and materials moved by water, rail, pipeline, and other modes of transportation does not compare to the dominant activity of trucks. According to the American Trucking Association (ATA), 9.9 billion tons of freight is moved annually across America and it takes more than three million truck drivers to accomplish this feat.

What is being moved?

A staggering 9.96 billion tons of freight is currently moving in the United States annually. The ATA shares these statistics about the vast and expansive reach of the trucking business:

• The trucking industry employs 7.1 million people in various types of trucking-related activities, as well as 3.5 million drivers.

• Truck drivers traveled 275 billion miles in 2013 and used 52.7 billion gallons of diesel fuel.

• In 2013, commercial trucks paid $37.3 billion dollars in federal and state highway user fees.

In addition, the United States Department of Transportation (USDOT) Bureau of Transportation Statistics reported in early 2014 that trucks carried 59.9 percent of all U.S.-North American Free Trade Agreement (NAFTA) freight and were the most heavily utilized mode for moving goods to and from (importing and exporting) Canada and Mexico, our NAFTA partners. It appears there is no dispute that trucking—a $700.4 billion industry in the United States in 2014--is a major force in our country's economy.

Where is it moving?

A lattice of highways forms the major inland network of freight distribution in the U.S. There are other major transport corridors along waterways, such as in New York and New Jersey, but the most active inland cities for freight distribution are Chicago, Detroit, Pittsburgh, Louisville, KY; Cincinnati and Columbus, OH; Charlotte, NC; Indianapolis, Kansas City, St. Louis, MO and Minneapolis, MN; Oklahoma City, Denver, CO; Salt Lake

City, UT; Atlanta, Phoenix, AZ; and El Paso, Laredo and Dallas, TX.

Who is doing the moving?

According to the USDOT, as of the end of 2013, there were 1.3 million carriers on file with the Federal Motor Carrier Safety Administration (FMCSA). This included 465,697 for-hire carriers, 725,179 private carriers and 168,680 other interstate motor carriers. Most of those in the latter group operate fewer than 20 trucks.

Almost every industry in America depends on the movement of freight by truck. Hospitals, pharmacies, retail stores, gas stations, grocery stores, and banks are just a few of the businesses that require frequent delivery by truck. Garbage disposal facilities, crude oil, petroleum and lumber products, construction materials suppliers, and the agricultural industry all depend on trucks to carry and deliver cargo imperative to business operations. Trucks haul materials through all stages of production from raw materials down to the finished product.

What is doing the moving?

The USDOT defines eight classes of vehicles that haul freight. Their classification is based on their gross weight vehicle rating (GWVR). For purposes of this publication, we focus on the larger 6 classes of vehicles, as classes 1 and 2 are made up of mainly passenger-type vehicles.

Medium-duty vehicles generally weigh between 10,001 pounds (GWVR) and 26,000 pounds and are in Classes 3 through 6. They include commercial vehicles such as local delivery trucks, ambulances, small buses and others.

Heavy-duty vehicles weigh from 26,001 pounds to 80,000 pounds and are Class 7 or Class 8 commercial vehicles. Class 8 is divided into two subgroups. Class 8a includes dump and refuse trucks, fire engines and city buses. Most tractor trailers are in Class 8b.

By comparison, the average weight of your average passenger vehicle on the road today is about 3,300 lbs. (even on the high end, many large SUVs weigh in at no more than 6,000 lbs.). So, getting hit by even the smallest of these commercial carriers, weighing in at three times the average vehicle, can create catastrophic damages. Even more alarming, imagine a fully loaded 18-wheeler weighing over 200,000 lbs. colliding with a compact vehicle or motorcycle. These large vehicles, by their sheer size, create an unparalleled danger to motorists.

Who regulates the industry?

Federal Regulation

Since 2000, the Federal Motor Carrier Safety Administration has been in charge of promulgating industry-wide regulations, covering the interstate activities of motor carriers from the pavement on up. These regulations include, but are not limited to, the following:

- exhaust emissions
- inspection protocols
- driver health and drive times
- mechanical condition of a vehicle

Before the rubber ever meets the road, the FMCSA determines how a driver becomes qualified to drive and maintains his or her qualification. Penalties for not following these regulations can be levied on the driver and the company he works for and some are very substantial.

State Regulation

While federal regulations govern interstate commerce, states may be inclined to develop their own sets of rules and regulations for businesses that operate solely within the state. An example may be a local bakery or newspapers that only make deliveries within the state boundaries.

Often, state regulations mirror those of their federal counterpart. However, when differences arise, federal regulations generally trump both state statutory law and even state common law.

What are the safety standards?

Maximum Drive Times

One of the top factors contributing to trucking accidents is driver fatigue. Drowsy driving decreases the ability to pay attention on the road, slows reaction time, and affects a driver's ability to make good decisions. Combine these dangers with a 200,000 lb. projectile traveling at a high rate of speed, and the likelihood for catastrophe increases exponentially. To make the industry as safe as possible, the FMCSA restricts and monitors the number of hours a truck driver may continue behind the wheel. In other words, they regulate the driver's "Hours of Service." There are different rules for drivers carrying property and drivers transporting passengers. The "Hours of Service" restrictions apply to the following:

• Trucks or tractor-trailers involved in interstate commerce even when the truck is empty

• Trucks weighing (including load) 10,001 pounds or more which have a GWVR or gross combination weight rating of 10,001 pounds or more

• Trucks transporting hazardous materials in a quantity requiring placards

The rule for driving with property is an 11-hour driving limit after starting out with 10 consecutive hours or more off duty. When the driver finishes the 11 hours, he may not drive again until 10 or more consecutive hours have passed since the end of the driver's last off-duty period.

Documentation

Truck drivers are required to keep a daily log of loads hauled, weight hauled, miles traveled, hours on duty, hours on duty not driving, consecutive days worked and other basic information.

As the trucking industry has evolved, so have the regulations on driving. After first being enacted in 1938, the controlling agencies have revised the rules time and again, with one constant in mind: minimizing driver fatigue and error due to excessive driving.

A driver's log book is a legally defined document which breaks a 24-hour day into 15-minute increments. In addition to the basic information (driver name, company information, etc.), the driver must specify when and where he stopped between shifts, and what duties the driver performed while on the clock. The driver must present the log book to federal or state authorities for inspection if requested and must retain his logs for six months.

Truckers must also have their vehicles regularly inspected and keep a record of the results of that inspection, as well as any resulting repairs.

Despite the dangers of fatigued driving, the hours-of-service regulations, and the strict requirements on documentation, drivers often disregard, or even falsify their records. This practice can even come at the recommendation or instruction of their employers, in their efforts to maximize profit.

Driving Requirements

A truck driver must meet pre-employment screening and licensing standards. Even after you become a driver, you must continue to adhere to the standards set forth by the federal and state regulators and can lose your right to operate the motor vehicles outlined above if you fail to do so.

Standards for Physical Health

The DOT requires the driver to undergo an initial physical, and re-examination every two years (more often if a driver has a condition such as high blood pressure which must still be within certain limits to drive). The driver must carry his medical examiner's certificate with him always to show that he has passed the driver's physical.

CDLs and Various License Endorsements

Commercial drivers must conform to certain regulations and maintain their Commercial Driver's License (CDL) if they legally operate any vehicle over 26,000 pounds or any vehicle that has air-operated brakes. The rigorous truck driver's test goes beyond the vision test, driver's skill test, age and insurance requirements the average automobile driver must meet to obtain a driver's license.

Each CDL applicant must pass knowledge and skills tests and meet minimum federal standards. The driver must answer 80 percent of the questions correctly to pass the test.

A driver may also be disqualified from holding a CDL for:

• Using a commercial vehicle in the commission of a felony involving manufacturing, distributing, or dispensing of a controlled substance. This infraction disqualifies one for life with no possibility of reinstatement.
• Serious traffic violations such as speeding more than 15mph, driving recklessly, making improper or erratic lane changes, following too closely, violating any

traffic control law in connection with a fatal accident and driving without a CDL.

Drivers are disqualified for 60 days for any second conviction within a three-year period of any combination of any offense committed in a commercial vehicle.

A driver is disqualified for one year for driving under the influence of alcohol or a controlled substance, or if he leaves the scene of any accident, or continues to operate a commercial vehicle after being disqualified.

• Railroad-highway grade crossing offenses. Penalties with this offense also become progressively more serious per number of infractions.

• Violating out-of-service orders such as when transporting placarded hazardous materials. The weight of this offense also increases with the number of infractions within a certain time.

There is no such thing as a "conditional" or "hardship CDL" or any type of limited driving privileges permitted to someone holding a CDL.

Any person who holds a CDL is considered to give their implied consent to any test of the driver being under the influence of alcohol or a controlled substance while on duty, operating, or in physical control of a commercial vehicle. Most companies give random tests while the driver is on duty. The trucker is notified to report to a nearby lab within a brief timeframe to be tested for drug or alcohol use or both.

For persons applying for a hazardous materials endorsement, the driver must meet standards for this endorsement specified by the Transportation Security Administration (TSA) and must also provide proof of citizenship and a Bureau of Citizenship and Immigration Services (BCIS) registration number if needed.

Truck drivers obtain various classes of CDL endorsements depending on the type of vehicle; whether it has a trailer; the type of material the truck carries, such as hazardous material; the type of brakes and the number of passengers.

Testing is often involved with many CDL endorsements. In addition, drivers who transport hazardous materials are required to placard their truck if carrying hazardous materials over a certain weight. This is to inform others that there are dangerous materials on board the vehicle.

Disqualification from Driving

If the state determines that an applicant has falsified information, or any of the required certification, the state shall disqualify a person from operating a commercial vehicle for at least 60 days. If the alleged fraud is in connection with the issuance of a license, the person must retake any test in which the authenticity of the results has been challenged within 30 days of notification of suspected fraud or be disqualified from holding a commercial license.

The FMCSA also has a 0.04% limit on blood alcohol concentration (BAC) levels. This compares to the 0.08% BAC limit for operation of non-commercial vehicles for drivers over 21 years of age in most states. Sanctions for alcohol-related driving violations may affect the driver's qualification and eligibility for both commercial and non-commercial licenses.

A driver must notify his employer within 30 days of any traffic violation conviction, except a parking citation. If a driver's license is suspended, revoked, disqualified, or cancelled, he must notify his employer by the end of the next business day following receipt of notice that action has been taken regarding his motor vehicle license.

Renewal Certifications

When the driver attempts to renew or update his CDL, the state must perform a check of the National Driver Registry (NDR) and the Commercial Driver's License Information System (CDLIS) to ensure the driver is not disqualified in that state or another jurisdiction and does not possess more than one commercial license.

The state must request the complete driving record of the driver from all jurisdictions where the driver has been employed for the past 10 years. The driver must also certify as to the type of operation he expects to conduct during the next licensing period and must submit a copy of his medical examiner's certificate to the state where his CDL is active ensuring he is physically qualified to operate a commercial vehicle.

Chapter 2
Trucking Accidents

Trucking Accident Statistics

In 2013, there were 30,057 fatal vehicle crashes in the United States, according to the Fatality Analysis Reporting System (FARS) published by the National Highway Traffic Safety Administration (NHTSA). Ohio claimed 990 of those fatalities, with 111 crashes involving trucks, and 38 of those, or 34%, were found to be caused by trucker error.

Large trucks accounted for eight percent of the vehicles involved in fatal crashes and 21 percent were drivers of light trucks.

Two percent of large trucks were in injury crashes in 2013 and three percent in property damage incidents. Of the

3,484 trucks in fatal crashes nationally, 74 percent were combination trucks, the FARS indicated.

The type of trucks involved in almost 4,000 injury crashes in Ohio in 2013, according to the Ohio Department of Public Safety (ODPS), were: 1,859 tractor/semitrailers; 940 single-unit two-axle trucks; 427 single-unit three-axle trucks; 312 single-unit trucks; 256 other medium/heavy vehicles; 82 bobtails (no trailer attached); 49 doubles and 5 triples.

The ODPS cited the following major causes of the accidents involving trucks where injury resulted:

- truck rollover
- trucker ran off road to the right
- equipment failure (blown tire, brake failure)
- trucker ran off road to the left
- trucker crossed centerline
- cargo loss or shift
- truck jackknifed

Overall, the number of people injured in crashes in Ohio decreased in 2013 and large truck fatalities declined for the first time since 2009, according to the NHTSA.

The Insurance Institute for Highway Safety (IIHS) emphasizes that trucks often weigh 20 to 30 times more than passenger cars. They are taller and have greater ground clearance. Thus, it should not be a surprise that, as the Institute points out, most of deaths in large truck crashes are drivers of passenger vehicles and their occupants.

It takes a loaded tractor-trailer 20 to 40 percent more distance to stop than a passenger car, therefore truck braking capability can be a significant factor in crashes especially on a wet, slippery road.

What happens after a trucking accident?

Investigation

If a trucker is involved in an accident while on duty, there are five things he or she should immediately do:

- Call the authorities.
- Take the proper steps regarding cargo, especially if it is hazardous and can damage the environment.
- Contact the employer.
- Contact the insurance company
- Take photos if possible.

If the accident is serious, the authorities should begin an investigation to determine who is at fault. Federal and state agencies will send a representative who is a certified truck inspector, or they will send a team of experts to review the condition of all significant mechanical parts of the vehicle involved. Perhaps, the manufacturer of a specific truck part may be implicated in the accident.

Alcohol and Drug Screening of Driver

Many times, a driver will have to submit to alcohol and drug testing immediately after a crash to determine if he or she was drinking or may have been using controlled substances at the time of the accident. This may be at the request of the authorities, or it may be pursuant to the policy of their employer.

Gathering of Evidence

The police will write a report about the accident noting the positioning of vehicles after the collision, any skid marks, any injuries and any road or inclement weather conditions that may have affected the accident. They will note if poor maintenance of tires may have resulted in a blowout or if the cargo may have been loaded improperly.

In addition to the police investigation and report, it may be necessary to employ the services of an accident reconstructionist with extensive experience and knowledge related to trucking accidents. While police are trained to investigate the scene, they are often not qualified to make determinations of causation, especially in the complicated fact sequences that often lead to trucking accidents.

In-Truck Recording Devices

Most trucks and some newer passenger cars have a "black box" or event data recorder (EDR) like those found in airplanes.

After a crash these small computer hard drive units can reveal such data as the speed patterns of the vehicle, the steering wheel angle, airbag deployment, engine performance level, when the driver used his brakes, how fast the driver was going, and how long the driver had been on the road. If there are cameras inside the truck, they can record activity in the cab and on the road in front of the vehicle.

The purpose of evaluating these various types of evidence is generally to demonstrate that the truck driver and the trucking company were or were not in compliance with government safety regulations. This evidence can also help piece together what was going on with the truck driver, vehicle and cargo in the minutes, hours and days before the accident.

This information can lead to important answers that were never previously available to accident investigators.

Truck and Vehicle Computers

After an accident, computers inside the truck can provide valuable information about the truck's maintenance and inspection history. Data from on-board communications systems and Global Positioning Systems (GPS) tracking units can also be downloaded.

Video Recording Equipment

Many commercial vehicles use video recording equipment to monitor their employees' activities while driving. These cameras often show the view looking into the cab of the vehicle, as well as the view from the driver's perspective. These cameras automatically record while the vehicle is on and can capture video evidence that would otherwise not be available. The cameras can show what a driver was doing immediately before an event (like dozing off or texting) and can be crucial evidence against a negligent carrier.

Preservation and Spoliation

Federal regulations require interstate carriers to maintain and preserve their records for a period of time. The destruction of documents, often referred to as "spoliation," can lead to sanctions against a trucking company. Moreover, it is important to request that the company keep all the above evidence for any potential claim against the carrier for negligence.

If the court finds spoliation has occurred, it may: 1) charge the jury that a rebuttable presumption has been created that the evidence would have been harmful to the defendant 2) exclude any testimony about the evidence, or 3) enter judgment against the party that tampered with the evidence. The severity of the court's sanction can increase if it is determined the party seeking sanctions was prejudiced because of destruction of evidence.

The trucking company may argue that the destruction of evidence was inadvertent and not deemed relevant to the plaintiff's case.

Because of this possible claim, plaintiff's lawyers are advised to send the defendant(s) a "letter of spoliation" as early as possible. It will detail certain items that are to be "maintained and preserved" and not "destroyed, discarded, changed, repaired or altered in any way."

The letter should state that the items are relevant to the plaintiff's cause of action and that all sanctions under the law will be pursued if evidence is destroyed.

Insurance Companies

When a commercial driver has an accident, especially a serious one, the insurance carrier for the driver and/or the owner company begins their involvement almost immediately. Even outside of regular business hours, drivers and owners contact their insurer, and an adjuster is assigned to the claim. Many insurance carriers have special hot lines or after-hours workers whose main purpose is to deal with large scale and/or catastrophic losses for their insureds.

These insurance companies and adjusters begin their internal investigation: requesting records, contacting supervisors, or even traveling to the scene. If the accident is serious enough, adjusters will contact local defense counsel to go to the scene to protect the driver and create attorney-client privilege. Remember, the insurance company is there to protect the driver and owner, NOT the parties injured by the negligent acts of those they insure.

Theories of Liability for an Accident

To establish liability and recover compensation, the plaintiff must first identify every individual, business entity, government official or insurance company who may have some responsibility in the truck accident or may be obligated to compensate the injured party.

Basic Negligence

Except for strict liability defective product cases, the plaintiff's theory in a truck accident will be based on negligence. Plaintiff must show defendant had a duty to drive safely, and breached that duty causing injury to the plaintiff. This is a simple concept that only requires the plaintiff to show that a reasonably prudent driver in the defendant's position would have acted with greater care.

Respondeat Superior

This is also referred to as "vicarious liability" and means that the trucking company is indirectly responsible for the accident based on its status as employer of the person responsible for the crash.

The motor carrier is only responsible for the driver's actions while the driver is acting within his scope of employment. A "respondeat superior" or "vicarious liability" claim is possible even if the company did nothing wrong.

A driver is acting within the scope of his employment if his activities further the carrier's business in any manner. If the driver departs on a personal mission, a carrier cannot be held vicariously liable for his actions in most situations.

Negligent Hiring

If the company knowingly hired a driver with substance abuse problems or a record of accidents, or failed to properly train the driver, the company may be liable for its own negligence in not researching the driver's background. Sometimes the negligent hiring action is taken against the insurance company.

Negligent entrustment is a similar charge and means that the trucking company should not have entrusted a vehicle to the driver because of his inexperience or inability to safely operate it. Negligent retention occurs when a trucking company discovers during the driver's employment that he is incompetent, or should be disqualified, but they retain him and allow him to drive a commercial vehicle.

Aggravated Circumstances

The shipper may be held liable if he participated in the loading process and the accident was related to improper loading of the vehicle. If the trailer is sealed before it is picked up by the carrier, it is presumed the shipper participated in the loading. Liability regarding the load can also extend to the driver, the owner of the vehicle, and the trucking company.

Federal regulations prohibit a trucking company from allowing a driver to operate a commercial vehicle while the driver's ability or alertness is impaired by fatigue, illness, or any other cause that would make driving unsafe.

A carrier has a duty to monitor its drivers' logs through a log verification procedure to ensure proper control of driving time in compliance with maximum hours of service regulations. These rules are established to prevent accidents caused by driver fatigue or inattentiveness. Any violation of these rules is admissible to prove negligence if an accident occurs.

Carriers should also monitor the speeds at which their drivers travel and if they are exceeding the speed limits. Many companies can easily do this by enabling a feature of the on-board "C-Link" which will automatically track the truck's speed.

Broker Liability

A broker is often "the middle man" between the shipper and motor carrier. He does not transport the load but deals with the shipper and motor carrier in arranging transportation.

The broker is not usually held liable on a theory of agency or vicarious liability but may be liable under a negligent hiring theory if he did not properly screen the motor carrier and failed to investigate the carrier's safety record.

Negligent Inspection, Maintenance and Repair

Federal regulations require motor carriers to inspect, maintain and repair all motor vehicles subject to their control and to keep all parts and accessories in safe and proper operating conditions always.

A trucking company must maintain the following records for each vehicle under its control:

• Identification of the owner and style of the vehicle

• A list of the nature and due date of various inspection and maintenance operations performed on the vehicle

• A record of inspections, repairs and maintenance performed

The records must be maintained for one year while the vehicle is housed or maintained by the carrier and for six months after the vehicle leaves the carrier's control. A carrier can be held responsible for any injury caused by its failure to inspect, maintain or repair any equipment under its control. Even a prior owner of a tractor-trailer can be held responsible for negligent maintenance of the vehicle in violation of federal safety regulations if an accident occurs.

Per Se Violations of Federal and State Regulations

The Federal Motor Carrier Safety Regulations (FMCSR) are a comprehensive list of guidelines and specifications governing the operation and maintenance of commercial vehicles.

Every interstate carrier is required to be knowledgeable about them and comply with all the provisions of the FMCSR applicable to that motor carrier's operations.

Every driver and employee must comply with the FMCSR. Equipment and accessories required by the regulations must be maintained in compliance with them. No one may aid, abet, encourage or require a motor carrier or its drivers to violate any safety regulation. A trucking company can be held liable for an injury resulting from its violation of the FMCSR.

As with other federal regulations, agencies in most states have adopted the FMCSR as applicable to any commercial vehicle operated within the state.

Texting and Cell Phone Use

Texting while driving is banned for all drivers in all 50 states, but federal law prohibits cell phone use and texting for all drivers of commercial vehicles in the U. S. The ban on texting includes GPS devices because the rules for commercial drivers prohibit unsafely reaching for a device, holding a mobile phone, or pressing multiple buttons to use or communicate on a device.

While driving, a commercial driver cannot dial a phone, e-mail, instant message, manually enter text into an electronic device or read from such a device.

According to the DOT, nearly 16,000 truckers were ticketed in 2013 for using their cell phones while driving. Truckers face civil penalties up to $2,750 for violating commercial rules on cell phone use while driving. Some also face immediate firing by their carriers who can be levied with substantial civil fines.

FMCSA researchers have found the odds of being involved in a safety critical event are 23.2 times greater for commercial drivers who text behind the wheel. At 55 mph, these drivers are taking their eyes off the road for an average of 4.6 seconds. Drivers who dial a cell phone while operating a vehicle are six times more likely to be involved in an accident, the researchers concluded.

Chapter 3

Insurance Coverage

Minimum Requirements for Coverage

Due to the size, weight and physical characteristics of most trucks, any truck accident is likely to result in severe injuries to those involved, not to mention significant property damage. Therefore, the minimum requirements for truck insurance are much higher than those for smaller vehicles and non-commercial drivers.

Federal law requires that interstate trucks carry minimum insurance coverage. State laws also mandate that trucks carry insurance. These requirements protect the victims of truck accidents from truckers and trucking companies that cannot afford to pay compensation to truck accident victims. Here are the minimum levels of financial responsibility for trucks:

Schedule of Limits - Public Liability

A.   Type of carriage:

For-hire (In interstate or foreign commerce, with a gross vehicle weight rating of 10,001 or more pounds)

Commodity being transported: Property (nonhazardous)

Liability limits: $750,000

B.   Type of carriage:

For-hire and Private (In interstate, foreign, or intrastate commerce, with a gross vehicle weight rating of 10,001 or more pounds)

Commodity being transported:

Hazardous substances, as defined in 49 CFR 171.8, transported in cargo tanks, portable tanks, or hopper-type vehicles with capacities more than 3,500 water gallons; or in bulk Division 1.1, 1.2 and 1.3 materials. Division 2.3, Hazard Zone A, or Division 6.1, Packing Group I, Hazard Zone A material; in bulk Division 2.1 or 2.2; or highway route-controlled quantities of a Class 7 material, as defined in 49 CFR 173.403

Liability limits: $5,000,000

C.   Type of carriage:

For-hire and Private (In interstate or foreign commerce, in any quantity; or in intrastate commerce, in bulk only; with a gross vehicle weight rating of 10,001 or more pounds)

 Commodity being transported:

Oil listed in 49 CFR 172.101; hazardous waste, hazardous materials, and hazardous substances defined in 49 CFR 171.8 and listed in 49 CFR 172.101, but not mentioned in (2) above or (4) below

Liability limits: $1,000,000

D.   Type of carriage:

For-hire and Private (In interstate or foreign commerce, with a gross vehicle weight rating of less than 10,001 pounds)

Commodity being transported:

Any quantity of Division 1.1, 1.2, or 1.3 material; any quantity of a Division 2.3, Hazard Zone A, or Division 6.1, Packing Group I, Hazard Zone A material; or highway route-controlled quantities of a Class 7 material as defined in 49 CFR 173.403

Liability limits: $5,000,000

Current insurance limits do not adequately cover catastrophic crashes, mainly because of increased medical costs. The decreasing real value of the current minimum levels of financial responsibility is effectively removing the function of insurance in covering catastrophic crashes.

From 1985 to 2013, the medical consumer price index (CPI) increased at a significantly higher rate than the core consumer price index (4.9 percent annually for medical care, compared to 2.8 percent for core). In fact, the medical consumer price index has outpaced overall inflation in all but one of those 29 years.

Endorsements

The prime way truckers meet financial responsibility requirements is through the purchase of insurance and by filing proof of insurance with applicable government agencies.

Whenever insurance is used in trucking operations to meet financial responsibility laws, the policies must be endorsed. These mandatory endorsements are certifications by the motor carrier's insurer that the policies meet requirements imposed by federal law.

For intrastate carriers and some private truckers not subject to federal regulation, equivalent state laws require insurance filings be made with a state authority such as the DOT.

One endorsement, a MCS-90 endorsement, is required to be part of any insurance policy issued to a motor carrier to comply with federal minimum insurance requirements. Promulgated by the Federal Motor Carrier Act of 1980, this act states that each motor carrier participating in interstate, for hire commerce, is required to show proof they have financial responsibility equal to or greater than minimums set by each state.

This endorsement requires the insurer to act as a surety for any injury to the public caused by the carrier during interstate transport and to be responsible for a judgment against the carrier.

Truck vs. Trailer Policies

The owner of a trailer may have a policy of liability insurance providing coverage to a driver as a permissive user. The permissive user should be listed on the insurance policy even if there are separate limits of coverage.

When the owner of a trailer is different than the tractor owner, a MCS-90 (see previous section) endorsement on the trailer's liability policy may be used to create an additional recovery up to the federal statutory minimum and expand the definition of a permissive user to include both the driver and the owner of the tractor.

Lessor's Coverage

The lessor (a person or company that leases property) of a tractor-trailer may purchase liability insurance to cover its vehicles even though the vehicles are leased to and operated by another company. The policy issued to the lessor may provide coverage to a permissive driver as an additional insured under the policy even though the lessor has no role in the transportation process and is not vicariously liable for the driver's conduct.

However, the lease agreement may limit the amount of coverage provided to the driver, so it is important for the driver to ask to see what insurance coverage he has under the lease if there is physical or cargo damage during the trip.

Traditional Coverage vs. Captive Coverage and Self-Insured's

Traditional

Traditional insurance is bought from an insurance company at competitive market rates. Some companies insure motor carriers, trucks and drivers through independent agents, others have sales staff.

Some specialize in specific niches such as large fleets, temperature-controlled equipment or owner-operators. Some cover only large operations, others handle thousands of small customers.

Self-Insured

Federal and state regulations require insurance coverage. A trucker must carry insurance to pay for any damage caused to another's property or medical care given to a person whose injury the driver caused.

Captive Explained

A "captive" is a special type of insurance company set up by a parent company, trade association or group of companies to insure the risks of its owner or owners and better manage its costs. Captives are essentially a form of self-insurance where the insurer is wholly owned by the insured and does not have to seek insurance in the commercial market.

Ohio businesses were not allowed to form captive insurance companies in the state until 2014. The "captive" is subject to state regulatory requirements and may be a major multinational corporation or a small nonprofit organization.

An Ohio captive may insure commercial multiple peril, ocean and inland marine, medical malpractice, workers compensation, commercial auto liability, and commercial auto physical damage and fidelity.

Self-Insured Retentions

Many liability insurance policies incorporate a provision under which the insured retains a portion of the risk. Common forms of significant risk retentions are large and matching deductibles and self-insured retentions (SIRs). These terms are often used interchangeably, but while they share similarities, there are key differences.

A deductible is defined as the portion of the loss to be borne by the insured before the insurer becomes liable for payment. Generally, under a primary deductible policy, the insurer must defend a claim from "dollar one." A deductible is an amount that an insurer subtracts from a policy amount, reducing the amount of insurance.

An SIR differs in that it is an amount an insured retains and covers before insurance coverage begins to apply. It is the amount not covered by an insurance company and that usually must be paid before the insurer will pay benefits. The insured must satisfy its SIR before the insurer is obligated to respond to the loss because SIRs come directly from the insured not the insurance company. Often the insured control how claims are handled.

Coverage Limits

In Ohio, a pure captive - that is any insurer that insures only the risks of its parent or affiliated companies of its parent - is required to possess and maintain a minimum of $250,000 in unimpaired capital and surplus.

Protected cell captives, captive insurance companies formed and licensed according to the Ohio Revised Code that insure or reinsure risks of separate participants, must possess and maintain a minimum of $500,000.

The participants in a protected cell captive have separate contracts that place each participant's liabilities into a protected cell.

Additional Insurance Coverage

Excess and Umbrella Policies

If a settlement in a claim is more than the policy limit, anything above that policy limit must be paid out of pocket by the trucking company if an excess or umbrella policy is not in force.

Excess liability coverage provides coverage above the limits of the underlying policy but offers no broader policy than that provided by the underlying document. Umbrella policies provide additional coverage sometimes not available in the underlying coverage. An umbrella policy is usually the more expensive of the two.

Excess liability coverage can be more restrictive than the underlying policy. When additional coverage is provided by the umbrella policy, it is usually subject to the insured assuming a deductible or a self-insured retention (SIR).

The limits provided in Excess and Umbrella policies can range from $1,000,000 to $5,000,000 and higher. The limits are dependent on the current value of protected assets and future-acquired assets.

Reinsurance Policies

Reinsurance is insurance purchased by an insurance company (the "ceding company") from one or more other insurance companies (the "reinsurer") directly or through a broker as a means of risk management. The ceding company and the reinsurer enter into a "reinsurance agreement" which details the conditions upon which the reinsurer pays a share of the claims incurred by the ceding company.

Passing off risk in this manner allows the ceding company to hedge against undesired exposure to loss and frees up capital to use in writing new insurance contracts.

A healthy reinsurance marketplace helps ensure insurance companies can remain financially viable, particularly after a major disaster such as a hurricane, because risks and costs are spread. Multiple insurance companies share risk by spreading risk.

With reinsurance the premium paid by the insured is typically shared by all the insurance companies so that an individual insurance company can take on clients who would be too great of a burden for a single insurance company to handle alone.

With all the possible layers of protection to make injury victims whole after a loss, it is important to do a completely thorough investigation of available coverage. You must know where to look and what to ask for to get the recovery you deserve.

Chapter 4
Procedure of Truck Accident Case

Accident Investigation

What the Insurance Company Has Already Done

As noted above, an insurance carrier begins its involvement in a loss almost immediately. They begin their investigation and defense of their insured, frequently without having many of the facts of loss or even any idea of who was at fault. They employ local defense counsel to create privilege and protect information that may be helpful to an injured party.

Insurance companies and their attorneys may make initial offers to settle claims with injured parties or their families without knowing many of the facts. They dangle seemingly large sums of money to minimize exposure to their companies and their insured.

Insurance companies and defense attorneys also know how expensive and time consuming it is to pursue a case to trial. They may even intentionally delay resolution of a case over a long period of time for this reason.

Sometimes they will go to enormous effort to fight a case or attempt to minimize the amount of damages being claimed. They may make a settlement offer on the lower end of the scale on the theory that the opposing attorney or injured party will not want to incur the substantial expense and investment of time going to trial.

What Evidence Do You Need?

You need to know what evidence the other side has in its possession.   What does the police report say? Was anyone cited in the accident? Who have the insurance companies spoken with? Were there witnesses to the collision?   Have any experts been retained by the opposition? Is there electronic evidence available such as video or computer data?

Complaint

To file a lawsuit, many documents must be provided to the court. A document called the "complaint" sets forth the facts that support the claim and provides a statement of the legal theories being alleged against the wrongdoer.

The complaint identifies the parties, the circumstances surrounding the accident and the specific laws that support the plaintiff's cause of action (the basis of the lawsuit).   The person filing the complaint is the plaintiff. The person being sued is the defendant.

A lawsuit is usually divided into the following stages: 1) the information-gathering or "discovery" stage 2) the pre-trial preparation stage   3) the pre-trial settlement or alternative dispute resolution stage and   4) trial.

In Ohio each court has its own local rules about filing deadlines and setting trial dates.   There are also numerous motions concerning issues of law that are often filed in a case and must be decided by the judge. These may involve discovery matters, or legal or evidence questions.

Discovery

After the lawsuit is filed, both sides participate in exchanging information about the case prior to trial in a process called "discovery."   This is a procedural device used to require the adverse party to disclose material facts and documents essential for the preparation of the requesting party's case. Often this is information that the other party alone knows or possesses.

Discovery narrows the issues of a lawsuit and can also promote the settlement of a lawsuit by providing the parties with opportunities to realistically evaluate the facts before them. The court must deny discovery if it is used in bad faith, or used to annoy, embarrass, oppress or injure the parties or the witnesses.

Privileged information such as confidential communications between an attorney and his client are matters that are not subject to discovery.

In Ohio the rules governing discovery are broad and allow each side much leeway in investigating evidence and witnesses that may be introduced at trial.

Even if the requested information may not appear directly relevant to the case, it may still be obtained if it can be shown it may lead to the discovery of relevant information.

Common Forms of Discovery or Practices Being Followed

Interrogatories

This involves sending and receiving answers to written questions posed to the opposing side. The number of questions asked may be limited depending on local court rules. There will be a specified time within which answers must be provided.

Request for Production of Documents

These are written requests for documents and other materials relevant to the claims made in the lawsuit. Again, each side has a certain amount of time to produce the asked-for documents.

Depositions

A deposition is a face-to-face meeting where attorneys ask questions of witnesses under oath and the session is transcribed. A deposition could last several hours.

Any witness who may offer testimony at trial may be deposed and the content of the deposition can be referenced during trial. The person's performance at the deposition can have great influence on the success or value of a case.

A lawyer may subpoena a person to produce documents or appear at a deposition or trial. The discovery phase may also include a request that a party submit to a medical or psychological examination to learn more about the person's health and help evaluate the person's claim for damages. A judge has considerable discretion to grant or deny this request.

Driver Logs and Related Testimony

Almost certainly the driver will be asked to present his logs for the time period surrounding the accident. The company he works for will be asked what measures it takes to verify the trucker's logs are accurate. If discrepancies are found here, this could be unfortunate news for both the driver and his company as keeping proper logs is a federal requirement.

Freedom of Information Act (FOIA)

The Federal Motor Carrier Safety Administration (FMCSA) has a "presumption of openness" and records on motor carriers can be requested through the federal DOT or state DOT. For additional information on the Freedom of Information Act, please visit the following online link:

https://www.transportation.gov/individuals/foia/freedom-information-act-foia-reference-guide

Additionally, company safety information is readily available online through the FMCSA at the following: https://www.fmcsa.dot.gov/safety/company-safety-records

Compliance

If one fails to comply with a discovery request, the other side can file a motion to compel compliance. The court considers the process of discovery to be a very serious matter.

Theories of Liability Developed Throughout

In general, if the truck driver is at fault in an accident:

• The driver could be found liable.
• The person or company who leased the truck or trailer could be liable.
• The manufacturer of the vehicle or the manufacturer of its tires or other mechanical parts may be found to have contributed to the cause and severity of the accident.
• The shipper or loader of the cargo, even the Department of Transportation can be found liable.

Trucking companies are held responsible for an accident caused by its driver if the driver was in the company's employ at the time of the accident and was engaged in an activity related to that employment.

However, if it can be proven the driver was carrying out an intentional act, or is an independent contractor, then the company may not be responsible. An independent contractor is a driver who does not have to strictly adhere to company policy.

For example, he will decide what route he will take and not have to follow someone else's instructions. He will also be responsible for safely maintaining the vehicle.

In any event, the insurance company may attempt to go after the trucking company assuming a large company will have deeper pockets and their client might receive a larger award.

Experts

A case will often require the assistance of expert testimony to help the attorney prove one or more elements of the action. The success of a case may hinge on the credibility or knowledge of the experts involved. It is important to furnish the expert with all the documentation necessary to form his or her opinion.

Sometimes the academic and professional credentials of the expert are extremely important. Other times the ability of the expert to teach and explain their field of expertise or technique to a jury or lay person may be valued more highly.

Attorneys must take into consideration the expense of hiring experts. It is a good idea to attempt to hire experts early in the case as the opposing attorney may have the same person in mind particularly when there are few qualified experts in a field.

During discovery, both parties will be required to provide a list of the expert witnesses they plan to call at trial. Expert testimony may be crucial in proving any number of additional xxx elements of your trucking accident claim. For example, if the injuries are permanent, it will be necessary to use an economist to provide evidence of lost earning capacity, or a life care planner to show the costs or any future medical expenses that may be necessary.

Another expert that may be helpful in a trucking accident case is one that is proficient in FMCSA standards. This expert can do a great deal in determining if log books are correct, if safety inspections were done according to protocol, and if maintenance is up to date. While basic negligence may be apparent, an expert can help identify other areas of concern that could help win or lose a case.

Accident Reconstruction

Results of accident reconstruction are often used by experts in cases involving fatalities and where there have been personal injuries.

Accident reconstruction is the scientific process of investigating, analyzing and drawing conclusions about the events that happened during a collision and what caused them to occur. It also includes visiting the accident site where measurements are taken.

The reconstruction process studies the role of the drivers, the vehicles, the roadway, the evidence left by the vehicles such as point of impact, final resting position, skid, scrub and gouge marks, and the environment where the accident happened. The laws of physics and engineering form the basis of reconstruction analyses and software may be used in calculations as well.

Inspection

Vehicle inspections are another typical part of an accident investigation. These inspections will usually include measuring the amount of damage and the damage profile of the vehicles. The profile is an analysis representing distinctive features of the vehicle and the damage profile measures how much that vehicle was displaced from its original profile.

The mechanical components of the vehicles such as brakes, steering, tires, suspension, lights, etc. may also be inspected and tested to determine if the condition of these components was a cause of the accident.

A pre-trip inspection should always be done before a truck begins hauling freight in interstate or intrastate commerce. After an incident, experts are sometimes asked to determine whether a malfunction was a contributing cause to an accident. It may have to be determined if a repair was properly executed. The maintenance history of the equipment should be reviewed to identify any trends or related maintenance issues.

Chapter 5
Do I Need a Lawyer?

Ohio law does not require you to hire a lawyer to pursue your personal injury claim. But that does not mean it is wise to proceed without one. Even the simplest case has its difficulties and challenges.

Within days, you may be contacted by insurance company representatives to obtain information regarding the crash and your injuries. Insurance representatives may even attempt to discuss settlement at that time – before you have a good grasp of what your medical condition is. To fully protect your rights, you should speak with an attorney before discussing the crash or your injuries with insurance representatives.

Insurance companies know how to defeat and minimize claims. They will work to protect their interests from the start, and it is generally a good idea to have a lawyer protecting your interests as well. Of course, the more serious your injuries are, the more important it is to have legal representation.

Other complicating factors may exist. For example, your health insurance providers may allege a "lien" against your injury claim, demanding the right to be repaid out of your claim for crash-related expenditures the insurers made on your behalf. Lien holders must meet certain legal requirements to prove their liens. And even assuming they do, you may have a right to a reduction of the lien amount. In other words, measures can be taken to protect your claim-related funds from third parties. Again, a competent injury attorney can help you navigate these issues.

Dealing with the aftermath of a trucking accident can be very stressful. On top of the emotional turmoil, physical pain, and disruption in your life, you have to deal with your property damage, medical treatment, the insurance companies, lien holders, legal issues, and a host of other matters.

A truck accident injury lawyer can help alleviate these burdens, so you can focus on what is most important – your recovery and getting back to living your life. A lawyer can also help level the playing field as you contend with well-financed insurance companies seeking to minimize your claim.

Chapter 6
Conclusion

What a person does immediately after a truck accident will depend on what kind of condition they are in. If they are unconscious, they will likely be taken to a hospital where they may or not recover consciousness. In the case of severe injury, others will have to make important decisions for the injured motorist.

If Someone is Injured in the Accident

Ohio law requires that you share insurance information and driver's license information at the scene with other drivers involved in an accident. You should record the location of the accident, the date, the other driver's insurance information and the names, addresses and phone numbers of any witnesses.

Do not talk to any insurance people at the scene who are from a company that does not represent you. Make statements only to the police and paramedics. If you cannot call the police or paramedics, ask someone to do it for you.

Do not move your car unless it is dangerous for it to remain on the roadway or wherever you are. If you leave things as they were when the accident occurred, this can help the police judge how the accident happened.

You will need to notify your insurance agent about the accident and may even call them from the scene but be careful about making any statements concerning fault even to your own insurance company. Your recovery of compensation could be jeopardized if you are too quick to take responsibility for an accident that may not be your fault or may only partially be your fault.

Even if you think you made a mistake, investigation of the accident may indicate otherwise. Police can sometimes cite the wrong party. Get a copy of the police report of the accident as soon as you can.

If the negligence of another person caused the accident, you may need legal help to proceed in recovering compensation for any injuries.

An injury lawsuit is not always a slam-dunk just because it looks like another party was negligent and caused the collision. Many insurance companies will try to put the other driver in a bad light.

You can probably see that you may need assistance with issues of this type, but many are reluctant to hire someone who has expertise in these matters. Not being represented by an attorney in your truck accident claim could cost you more in the long run.

Other Things to Watch Out For:

• Agreeing to give a recorded statement to an insurance company. This can be used against you at a later time. So, be very careful about making any type of statements.

• Requests to sign an authorization permitting the insurance company to gather records about you—your medical history, etc. Signing such an authorization allows them to invade your privacy and obtain information they normally would not have access to. Again, they will try to use it against you.

• If an insurance company advises you that you don't need an attorney, they are saying they don't want you to retain one because it is not in the insurance company's best interest. They are not worried about your best interest.

• If they offer you a quick settlement or hand you a check before you have even mentioned compensation, don't accept it. They are trying to get off cheaply and you likely deserve and can obtain much more.

•   Trying to befriend you. Some will try to win your trust and make you believe that you are being treated fairly. Then they will "lowball" you on your personal injuries, offering far less than you should receive in hopes that you will take the underpayment because they have been so "nice."

You should contact an attorney as soon as there is any potential you need legal help. You can guarantee the insurance companies have already started working on their claims so there is no reason to delay.

You can contact Slater & Zurz LLP in many ways. Call us at 1-800-297-9191 or e-mail slaterzurz@slaterzurz. You can also reach us via our website at slaterzurz.com.

The Authors

The Ohio law firm of Slater & Zurz LLP is a team of legal professionals dedicated to helping victims of all types of accidents and their families throughout Ohio. The law firm has been entrusted to handle more than 40,000 personal injury cases and has helped clients receive more than $150 million in settlements and verdicts.

Attorney Jim Slater is the managing partner of Slater & Zurz LLP and has been actively practicing law for over 40 years. When Mr. Slater is asked what the law firm of Slater & Zurz LLP does, he replies simply by saying:

We Make Others Do What They Do Not Want To Do.

We make the decision makers at insurance companies pay fair and proper compensation to victims of accidents.

We make individuals and businesses pay their customers and employees the money they owe them.

We provide comfort to families by financially punishing owners of nursing homes that harm their loved ones.

We convince juries to award our clients the money they deserve.

In all cases, we work tirelessly to be sure our clients get what they are entitled to receive.

Prior to asking for our help, our clients were either denied proper compensation or were uncertain whether they could receive the compensation they deserved.

We have made companies pay millions when they negligently manufactured products that caused serious injuries.

We have made insurance companies pay hundreds of thousands of dollars when the dogs of homeowners they insured attacked innocent children and caused serious injury.

We have made a hospital pay millions when one of its doctors caused a child's death.

We made a large company pay millions to its employees when the company failed to pay commission income they earned.

At Slater & Zurz LLP all cases do not involve millions or hundreds of thousands of dollars. Many of our cases involve smaller amounts of money. But there is a common theme. We make companies and people who have treated or would treat our clients unfairly do what they do not want to do.

This is what we do at Slater & Zurz LLP. This is what we have done for over 40,000 clients over 40-plus years. I am personally proud of the difference we make for our clients. It has been our goal, from the beginning, to make people proud that we are their attorney and pleased with the results we obtain for them. This is what they tell us daily.

James W. Slater

Free Consultations Are Always Offered at

Slater & Zurz LLP

Attorneys at Law

Serving Clients Throughout Ohio

From These Office Locations:

Akron • Canton • Cleveland • Columbus

Please call toll free

1-800-297-9191

or visit slaterzurz.com

or ohiotruckingaccidents.com

More Free Books Available from Slater & Zurz LLP

We have written books on many different legal topics including the following:

When A Dog Bites Fight Back

Stop Nursing Home Abuse in Ohio

Motorcycle Crashes in Ohio

Legal Malpractice in Ohio

A Wrongful Death in Ohio

To request a free copy of any of our books, please call 1-800-297-9191 or send us a message from our website at slaterzurz.com.